DANIEL DEFOE'S

ROBINSON CRUSOE

A GRAPHIC NOVEL

BY MARTIN POWELL
& EVA CABRERA

RAINTREE
A CAPSTONE COMPANY
PUBLISHERS FOR CHILDREN

Raintree is an imprint of Capstone Global Library Limited, a company incorporated in England and Wales having its registered office at 7 Pilgrim Street, London, EC4V 6LB – Registered company number: 6695582

www.raintree.co.uk
myorders@raintree.co.uk

Text and illustrations © Capstone Global Library Limited 2016.

British Library Cataloguing in Publication Data
A full catalogue record for this book is available from the British Library.

Paperback ISBN: 978-1-4747-0388-8
Ebook ISBN: 978-1-4747-0393-2

19 18 17 16 15
10 9 8 7 6 5 4 3 2 1

Back matter written by Dr Katie Monnin

Designer: Alison Thiele

Printed in China.

CONTENTS

A REAL-LIFE CASTAWAY

Published in 1719, Daniel Defoe's *Robinson Crusoe* tells the story of a man stranded on a desert island after a shipwreck. It is a work of fiction, but some of the elements of the classic tale were inspired by a real-life castaway called Alexander Selkirk, a buccaneer (or pirate) who voluntarily chose to live on a deserted island.

Selkirk and his shipmates visited an island called Más a Tierra in October 1703. When they were ready to depart, Selkirk deemed the ship unseaworthy and chose to stay behind, alone on the island. As Selkirk had predicted, the ship later sank, killing most of the crew in the process.

Because of the shipwreck, Selkirk was able to gather a number of useful supplies from the wreckage, including a musket, gunpowder, tools and clothing. He lived on the island for over seven years by creating shelter, hunting the local game and collecting rainwater.

A ship finally came to Selkirk's rescue on 2 February 1709. Selkirk's real-life adventures are said to have heavily influenced Daniel Defoe's *Robinson Crusoe*. Because of the book's huge popularity over the next two centuries, the island of Más a Tierra was renamed Robinson Crusoe Island in 1966.

Some would argue that Alexander Selkirk was more deserving of the honour, but the fact that he was a pirate (and returned to his thieving ways after being rescued) might have influenced the decision to honour the fictional Robinson Crusoe instead.

DUNDEE

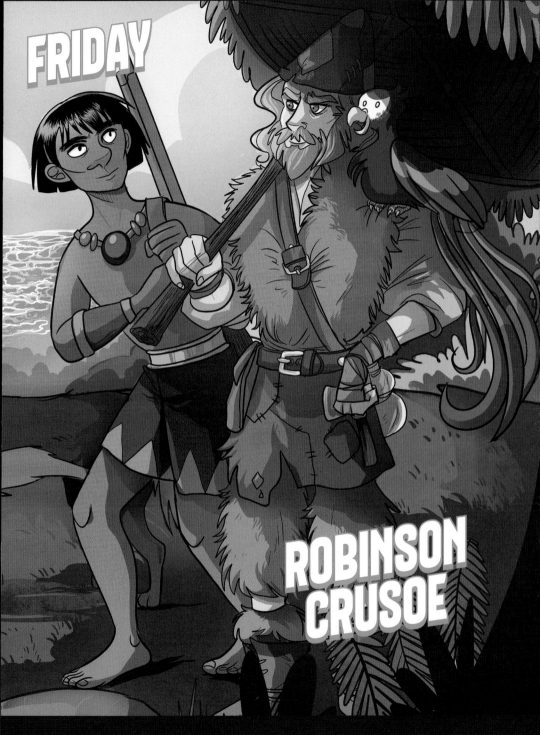

FRIDAY

ROBINSON CRUSOE

CHAPTER 1

THIRST FOR ADVENTURE

I am Robinson Crusoe, born in 1632, in the city of York.

As the son of a successful merchant, I was given a fine education. My father encouraged me to start a career in law.

For as long as I could remember, everything had been planned out for me. Certainly, I had everything I ever needed.

And yet, all I ever wanted was to go to sea.

My father disapproved of my thirst for adventure.

Just one sea voyage, Father. That's all I ask.

Absolutely not. I forbid such nonsense.

But Father, please...

Enough. It's time you grew up. Think of more practical occupations.

Knowing my mother could sometimes change my father's stubborn mind, I spoke to her one quiet evening.

All I want is to see other parts of the world.

It would be better to have Father's approval.

It's not fair.

Your father is reminded of your older brother. He went off to war and never returned home.

You're all we have left, Robinson.

Please stay here with us.

Because the journey would last only a few short weeks, I left without saying farewell to my parents.

I knew they would gravely disapprove.

It was wonderful to finally be at sea.

Little did I realize that I was beginning the adventure of a lifetime.

Before long, I had my first experience of a terrifying storm. The most frightful waves attacked the ship.

Mountains of sea water hurled at us with fury.

I was certain we were doomed.

The ship began to sink. We escaped in the lifeboats just in time.

CHAPTER 2
SAVED

Soon a passing ship rescued us. They brought us to port in London. The townsfolk were very generous.

A few days later, I met Daniel's friendly father.

This blanket will keep you warm. Come home and have supper with us.

Take my advice, my boy.

The fearsome fate of your first voyage was a warning. You should go home to your family.

I cannot do that, sir. Everyone would laugh at me. They'd call me a coward.

Better to be a living coward than a dead fool, no?

It's impossible to go home until I've proven myself.

Very well. I admire your spirit, young man.

Please take this money. I hope that it will help you.

Thank you, sir.

I stayed in London for several days. The allure of the sea continued to call to me.

Luck was with me, for I met the captain of a merchant ship.

I'd hoped for a more experienced sailor, but I'm willing to take a chance on you, Mr. Crusoe.

I'm grateful, Captain.

Here's to a successful voyage for both of us!

In spite of my past misfortunes, I was cheerful and excited about beginning my next journey.

The captain was a fine instructor. He taught me the rules of navigation.

You've learnt very quickly, Mr Crusoe. I'd say you are a natural-born sailor.

Thank you, Captain. I do love the sea.

However, the dangers of the sea are many.

Once again, fate frowned upon me.

The pirates swarmed on board in a storm of flashing steel and exploding gunpowder.

The captain was killed.

The fiends took the ship. We survivors were kept captive for over two miserable years.

Finally, one dark night, I managed to escape in a longboat.

Although I didn't realize it at the time, I was not far from the east coast of South America.

I'd had enough adventure at that point, so I settled on a plantation in Brazil.

But I had not lost my yearning for the sea.

An opportunity came four years later. The captain of a merchant ship offered me passage on a voyage to Africa.

You and Dundee seem to be friends, Mr Crusoe. He's not nearly so nice with the rest of the crew.

Perhaps this means we'll have good luck on our journey, Captain.

Judging by the stormy sky, we'll need all the luck we can get.

The captain's words echoed inside my mind as the full horror of the hurricane blasted us.

Then a mountainous wave pitched us into the angry heavens.

I lost consciousness.

When I awoke...

CHAPTER 3
STRANDED

...Miraculously, I was safe and sound on a lonely beach.

I searched for my friends, but I found no one.

The storm had anchored the sinking ship upon the reef.

It loomed there as silent as a tomb.

I was alone.

I explored my new world.

Fearful of predators, I selected a tall tree.

I slept settled safely in its lofty branches for the night.

The following morning, I enjoyed a coconut breakfast.

My jackknife was my only possession in the world.

I felt fortunate for that, though I knew my situation was grim.

If I was going to survive, I needed much more.

I swam out to the wrecked ship.

With some difficulty, I climbed aboard.

Everything had been washed overboard during the storm.

But I felt certain that the cargo below was safe and intact.

It was eerie all alone on the silent ship. My nerves were on edge.

I felt haunted by the ghosts of my former shipmates.

Every shadow seemed alive.

I struggled to prevent my imagination from going wild.

Suddenly…

GRRRR

BARK!

Dundee! I'd forgotten all about you!

My spirits were lifted.

Good dog, good boy. I'm happy to see you, too.

I constructed a basic raft and returned to the beach with all the provisions I could pack.

The ship's cats were less excited about joining me, but I eventually persuaded them to come.

The new tools, rifles and gunpowder encouraged me.

Together, Dundee and I set off on our first exploratory mission.

Well, there's no doubt about it.

We're on an island, all right.

I made my camp near the beach. That way, I could see any passing ships that might appear.

Then I created a calendar by carving a notch on a piece of wood every day.

The rainy season was on its way. I began to work on a shelter to protect me from the elements.

It was hard work, but I was happy to keep busy.

Carving out a small cave for use as a storm shelter was gruelling. But it, too, helped pass the time.

I finished just as the storms came.

WHOⓄⓄⓄⓄ

They howled outside the cave in frightful torrents.

During the unending rain, I developed a fever.

I felt as though I was dying.

My only distraction was a worn bible I had found on the ship.

As the weather improved, so did my health.

Dundee and I continued our exploration of the island.

I can hardly believe my eyes!

Look, Dundee! An abundance of fruit!

All we could ever eat – and more!

My days were busy.

I hauled the fruit back to my camp. I taught myself to make cheese from the goat's milk.

I even taught myself to sew new garments from leather.

I was so busy that I almost didn't notice an important date.

It's hard to believe...

...but I've been on this island for a whole year.

I tried my hand at gardening using a bag of spilled chicken feed from the wrecked ship.

Seed-bearing plants soon began to sprout!

Within a few months, I'll be able to make fresh bread!

Some weeks later, I started to feel restless.

I decided to complete my exploration of our island.

Soon...

Look at that, Dundee! I've never seen anything like it!

Rejuvenated, I set to work making a sturdy wooden bowl.

But my proudest achievement was the oven I built for baking bread.

I knew nothing about baking, and made many mistakes.

But I had all the time in the world to get it right!

Not bad, eh, boy?

The years blurred together. I experienced long periods of loneliness.

I don't think anyone's coming to rescue us, Dundee.

I decided to take fate into my own hands.

I tamed a parrot to keep me company. Sadly he wasn't much for conversation.

SQUAWK!

My companions watched with great curiosity as I carved a great cedar tree into a canoe.

It was a massive job. I spent half of the year working on it.

When it was finally finished...

ARF!

Don't worry, boy! It's just a test voyage!

I'll be back soon!

?

My plan was simple: sail around the island to test the boat.

However, steering the boat proved much harder than I'd anticipated.

The powerful current pushed me further and further out to sea.

Crusoe!
Crusoe!
Squawwwk!

The parrot had finally learnt how to talk.

I laughed until I was exhausted.

I decided that I'd had enough adventures.

For the next nine years, I lived a quiet life on the island.

One sunny day, while strolling along the beach, my life changed forever…

What have you found, Dundee?

SNIFF SNIFF

No…

…It can't be…

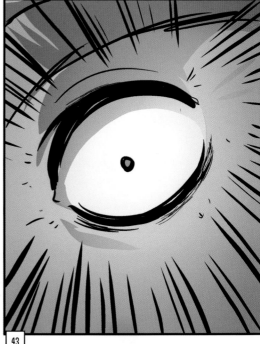

I became overwhelmed with terror.

I didn't sleep that night.

I wondered if people from another island had invaded. I'd heard of cannibals inhabiting this part of the world…

The following morning, I loaded all of my muskets. I set to work building a more secure fortress.

For many months, I remained on my guard. I didn't see any further signs of other human beings.

Two years later, everything changed.

There was no doubt about it. They were cannibals, just as I'd feared.

They were going to execute a man on the beach.

I couldn't let that happen.

click!

They froze in horror. I reasoned that they'd never heard a gunshot before.

BLAM

Even though they were cannibals, I did not aim to kill.

Dundee fought bravely at my side.

THUD

That gave me the instant I needed to rush them, using my empty rifle as a club.

Luckily, my foes quickly retreated back into the sea.

It's all right. You're safe now.

One day, Dundee died at a very old age.

Friday mourned him as much as I did.

I'd never had a more faithful friend than Friday. He was a friendly, intelligent and eager to learn companion.

Friday was fascinated with the guns. After all, they had saved his life.

Almost immediately, he was a much better shot than I.

BLAM

Excellent, Friday!

Apart from target practice, we lived a quiet, peaceful life.

Until...

Robinson! Strangers are coming!

We raced towards the beach.

We must keep out of sight.

These men could be friends ... or foes.

CHAPTER 7
MUTINY

What did you see?

That British vessel shouldn't be in these waters.

Something is very wrong, Friday.

A longboat glided to our beach, carrying a dozen cruel men. They had a few prisoners bound in rope.

From cover, we watched with our fingers on the triggers.

Bad men, yes?

Very bad men, Friday.

Soon, they vanished into the jungle in search of fresh water.

We decided to approach them.

Eh? Who's there?!

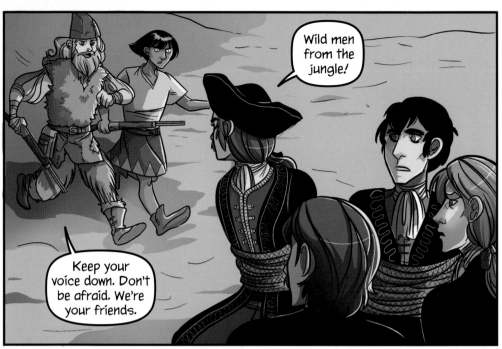

The mutineers immediately fired on us. We had no choice but to shoot back.

BLAM

BLAM

BLAM

The resulting explosion of gunfire on both sides was like a thunderclap.

Strike swiftly before they can reload!

THUD

The fight was over very quickly. The surviving mutineers surrendered.

We'll hide here and wait for some to come ashore.

Together, we made plans to take back the captain's ship.

Then we'll ambush them.

It happened exactly as we'd planned. All but two of the men came ashore and entered the jungle.

The two guards on the boat gave up without a fight.

Then we waited for the others to re-emerge from the jungle.

It was a tense moment; the odds were against us...

BLAM

Chaos reigned.

SWIPE!

These men had brought war to our peaceful island.

ACK!!

61

It was a fight we had to win.

Finally…

Don't shoot! We give up!

We surrender!

Thank you, sir. You saved my life and those of my crew.

I am eternally grateful.

Later, after nightfall, the captain and his loyal crew glided to their stolen ship.

They were determined to win it back.

The captain ordered Friday and me to stay behind. He said we'd done enough already.

We waited anxiously to see which flag would be raised.

At dawn, we got our answer.

Look, Friday! They've raised their own flag!

The ship is theirs again!

Friday and I departed for England, given new clothing by the ship's friendly crew.

All I brought with me was the parrot, my old cap and the umbrella. Souvenirs of my great adventure.

I had lived upon the island for twenty-eight years, two months and nineteen days.

ABOUT THE AUTHOR AND ILLUSTRATOR OF THIS RETELLING

Martin Powell has been a freelance writer since 1986. He has written hundreds of stories, many of which have been published by Disney, Marvel, Tekno Comix, Moonstone Books, Stone Arch Books and others. In 1989, Powell received an Eisner Award nomination for his graphic novel *Scarlet in Gaslight*. This award is one of the highest comic book honours.

Eva Cabrera is a sequential artist born in Jalapa, Veracruz, Mexico. She is an Art Director and also illustrates comic books for a living. She has won several comic-related national contests and has participated in various art expos.

GLOSSARY

cannibal a person who eats the flesh of human beings

coward someone who is not at all brave or courageous

forbid to order someone not to do something

grim unpleasant or worrying

grueling requiring great effort

mourned showed great sadness over someone's death

mutiny a situation in which a group of people, like sailors or soldiers, try to take control away from the person who commands them

paradise a very beautiful, pleasant, or peaceful place that seems to be perfect

reef a long line of rocks or coral or a high area of sand near the surface of the water in the ocean

yearning feeling a strong desire for something

READING QUESTIONS

1. What does Robinson Crusoe do before he boards the ship that ultimately sinks in a storm? How does Crusoe feel about the captain of the ship?

2. Describe the storm that ultimately destroys the ship. And, moreover, how Crusoe manages to survive.

3. How does Robinson Crusoe change over the years he spent on the deserted island? Find five examples of change in his appearance, personality, or perspective.

WRITING PROMPTS

1. What are some ways someone could survive on a deserted island? Consult multiple resources (the internet, texts from the library, or teachers). Then write about how you would survive on a desert island.

2. Write a list of activities you would do if you and Friday were friends and stranded on the deserted island in this book.

3. In a couple of paragraphs, explain what you think Robinson's most challenging experience is on the island.

READ THEM ALL!

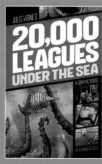

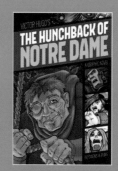

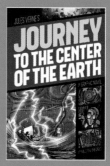

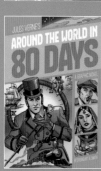

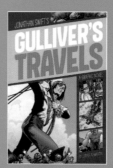

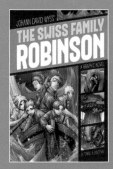

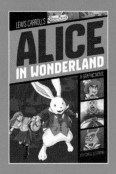
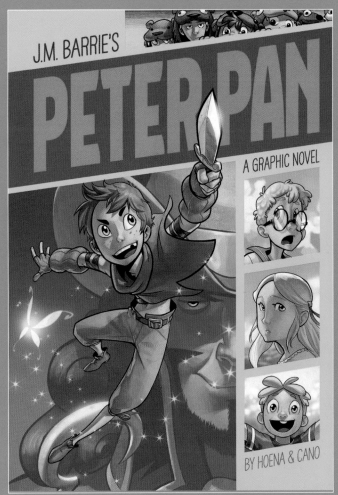

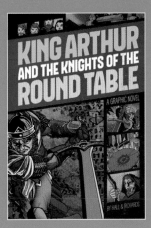